by Sharyn Squier Craig

A Fun Way to Frame Quilt Blocks!

CHITRA PUBLICATIONS

Copyright © 1996 by Sharyn Squier Craig

All Rights Reserved. Published in the United States of America
Printed in China

Chitra Publications
2 Public Avenue
Montrose, Pennsylvania 18801

No part of this publication may be reproduced or transmitted in any form or by any means, electronic or mechanical, including photocopy, recording, or any information storage and retrieval system now known or to be invented, without permission in writing from the publisher, except by a reviewer who wishes to quote brief passages in connection with a review written for inclusion in a magazine, newspaper, or broadcast.

Fifth printing: 2002

Library of Congress Cataloging-in-Publication Data

Craig, Sharyn Squier, 1947-
      Twist 'n turn: a fun way to frame quilt blocks! / by Sharyn
  Squier Craig.
        p.   cm.
      ISBN 1-885588-10-0
      1. Patchwork. 2. Patchwork quilts. I. Title.
TT835. C73323 1996   96-23733
746.46--dc20   CIP

Editor: Nancy Roberts
Design and Illustration: Susan Barefoot
Cover Photography: Guy Cali & Associates, Inc., Clarks Summit, PA
Inside Photography: Ken Jacques Photography, San Diego, CA

Introduction
How it Began 4
Save the Day with Twist 'n Turn 4
Start Big with a Triple Twist 5
Help from the Quilt Photos 5

Photo Gallery of Twist 'n Turn Quilts 6

Chapter 1
Getting Started 8

Photo Gallery of Twist 'n Turn Quilts 10

Chapter 2
Twist 'n Turn Method 1:
    Using Rectangles 11

Photo Gallery of Twist 'n Turn Quilts 13

Chapter 3
Twist 'n Turn Method 2:
    Using Triangles 14

Photo Gallery of Twist 'n Turn Quilts 17

Chapter 4
Twist 'n Turn Method 3:
    Using Templates 18

Photo Gallery of Twist 'n Turn Quilts 20

Chapter 5
A Triple Twist Exercise 22

Photo Gallery of Twist 'n Turn Quilts 25

Chapter 6
Thoughts on Setting 27

Photo Gallery of Twist 'n Turn Quilts 29

Chapter 7
Twist 'n Turn Block Library 30

INTRODUCTION

Welcome to a fun new way to frame your quilt blocks! If you've been looking for a way to set blocks that's a little bit different and extremely easy, then look no more. You'll really enjoy what can happen to your quilts once the blocks start twisting and turning. All you do is sew rounds of fabric strips or pieces to the sides of blocks to tilt them for a lively new look. You can even equalize block sizes this way, making it possible to use different sized blocks together in a quilt.

Part of the fun is that you can interpret the "Twist" yourself. Add one round for a Single Twist, two for a Double Twist and three for a Triple Twist. There is no single "right way."

In this book you get lots of photos that illustrate the Twist 'n Turn design concept plus how-to's for three different methods you can use to create the look in your quilts. You'll use rectangular strips for framing the blocks in Method 1 and oversize triangles in Method 2. In Method 3, you'll draft and create exact templates for the triangular framing pieces. You'll also learn the pros and cons of each method so you can choose the one that will work best in your quilts. And when you try the Triple Twist Exercise you'll use two of the methods and become a master of Twist 'n Turn!

How it began

The fun started for me in 1991. When I retired from teaching quilting in adult education classes, my students presented me with a box full of "six-inch" blocks...148 of them to be exact. There's a reason for the quotation marks around "six-inch." Those blocks actually ranged from 4 1/2" up to 8" square. Mind you, they weren't supposed to be different sizes. I faced two challenges. One was how to use so many different sized blocks. The other was to integrate the diverse block patterns and fabric colors. Mixing complex pieced blocks such as the Feathered Star with simple ones such as the basic Nine Patch would be a real challenge.

I knew that sewing straight strips around each of the blocks and then squaring them up would make it obvious that the blocks were different sizes. Rather than calling attention to that fact, I preferred to create a quilt in which each block could be seen individually while at the same time read as a "whole." My solution was to Twist 'n Turn the blocks and I came up with the design idea for "Challenges and Resolutions" (page 6).

Usually I know where the visual stimulation comes from for any of my design ideas. But with Twist 'n Turn, I don't remember. It may have been from seeing a quilt in a magazine years earlier and "filing" the image away. It's related to the Twisted Log Cabin block. Maybe I had seen one of those at a recent quilt show. The fact is that I don't recall and it really doesn't matter. I'm convinced that "Someone" is out there sprinkling fairy dust around the quilt world so that many quilters start playing with the same idea at the same time!

Since creating "Challenges and Resolutions" from those unequal sized blocks in 1991, I have seen other similar quilts. Each one is a bit different in the way the blocks are framed, the colors, setting or borders. In fact, they differ in just about every way possible. But one thing they all seem to have in common is a whimsical quality which makes each one positively come alive!

Save the Day with Twist 'n Turn

Twist 'n Turn has saved blocks that seemed beyond salvation. For example, I originally thought the angular, exploding star blocks in "Celebration" (page 17) were too strong to be used together in a quilt. This can be a common problem with the blocks in sampler quilts. When they were placed on the flannel wall it

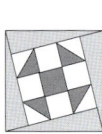 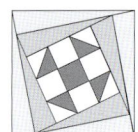 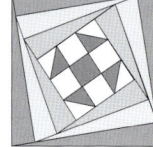

was hard to know just where to focus. To counter-balance the intensity of the individual stars, I selected strong colors to frame the blocks. Once I began auditioning different fabrics on the design wall, I moved from disliking the blocks to loving the way they were shaping up in the quilt.

The Ohio Star blocks in "Saturday Night Live" (on the cover and page 21) were leftover blocks from a 1985 opportunity quilt. Quilters from all over San Diego County sent 6" Ohio Star blocks. I used them in a fundraiser quilt for the first Quilt San Diego Visions exhibition. More than 300 blocks were sent in, again ranging from 4 1/2" to 8" square. I used 165 blocks in the quilt and then used 140 more to make several smaller fundraiser quilts. But some blocks were left that just never seemed to "fit." Ten years after the charitable project, "Saturday Night Live" was "born" by twisting and turning those leftover blocks!

Start Big with a Triple Twist

"Saturday Night Live" was my first Triple Twist quilt using Twist 'n Turn. I recommend using the Triple Twist if your blocks are not all the same size or if they are smaller than 8" square. Because the Triple Twist can double the block size, it's also a good choice if you don't have many blocks but you want a larger quilt. My original 6" Ohio Star blocks "grew" to 12" square once they were framed. So be advised about the growth factor! You probably wouldn't select the Triple Twist if you started with 12" blocks. (Notice I said probably rather than never. No rules!)

The Triple Twist is also a fun way to play with color. The middle round on the block looks great in a light value or bright fabric. It provides a perfect opportunity to add a little zest to otherwise ho-hum blocks. Do keep in mind that a little goes a long way when using light or bright fabrics, so I recommend using narrower strips for the second round.

I suggest that you start with the Triple Twist Exercise after reading over the three methods. It's a good way to experiment with both Methods 1 and 2 for framing your blocks. It relies on a very efficient and organized system and there is very little fabric waste.

Another idea is to "practice" any of the framing methods using squares of novelty printed fabric instead of a pieced block. Quiltmaker Carol O'Brien did just that with a Dalmatian print (page 7). This way of learning the technique can also be a quick way to stitch a baby quilt for the cuddle quilt projects so many quilters are involved in. Just cut 6" squares of your favorite novelty fabric and you're ready to Twist 'n Turn!

Help from the Quilt Photos

As you look at the quilts in this book, notice that some designs look very controlled, while others are more free. You can achieve control by choosing the direction the blocks twist and turn. You can also create a more or less controlled look by your choice of fabric colors. For example, do you want to use one fabric all the way around? (See "Challenges and Resolutions" on page 6 and "Old Shoes" on page 29.) Or do you want to use different fabrics on each side of the blocks? (See "New Shoes" on page 29 and "Starring the Best Friends" on page 10). Control could even mean using strips that are all the same color but cut from lots of different fabrics. (See "The Asilomar Sampler" on page 13.) As you Twist 'n Turn, you'll find that you can write your own rules. Now that's design freedom!

Also notice quilts which first use straight strips to frame the blocks before using the "twisting" pieces. In "My Quilting Friends" (page 17) I sewed three rounds of straight strips around each block before twisting them. Blocks in "Starring the Best Friends" (page 10) got one straight accent strip sewed to the sides first, but using two different colors for them made the blocks appear more twisted. Straight strips can also be used for sashing. "The Asilomar Sampler" (page 13), "Celebration" (page 17) and "Starring the Best Friends" all have straight-strip sashing between the Twist 'n Turn framed blocks.

Your favorite method and how you use Twist 'n Turn is entirely up to you. Just have fun while you're making wonderful new quilts. Go get some of those friendship exchange blocks or block-of-the-month winnings from the back of your closet and start sewing! You'll be so glad you did.

Sharyn

Here's the quilt that started it all! Sharyn used Twist 'n Turn to frame 144 gift blocks from her adult education students in **"Challenges and Resolutions."** The blocks were supposed to measure 6" square but actually varied in size. By framing them, Sharyn was able to make them fit together in a quilt.

Carol O'Brien of Ramona, California, cut 6" squares of a novelty print fabric for her **Dalmatian quilt**. She framed the squares in red and black to make a truly quick and easy baby quilt.

Bright colors and randomly twisting blocks give Margaret Reap's **Sampler quilt** a lively, happy feel. The El Cajon, California, quilter chose a Triple Twist to frame the blocks.

The Gallery

Chapter 1

GETTING STARTED

Triple Twist, cut four 2 1/2" strips and six 3 1/2" strips. For 20 blocks, cut at least fourteen 2 1/2" strips and twenty-seven 3 1/2" strips.

Methods 1 and 2 require strips of fabric. Assuming blocks measure between 4 1/2" and 12 1/2", I recommend starting with strips no narrower than 2 1/2" and no wider than 3 1/2". Frame a sample block with a 2 1/2" or 3 1/2" strip. Once you see the result, you can adjust strip widths according to your preference.

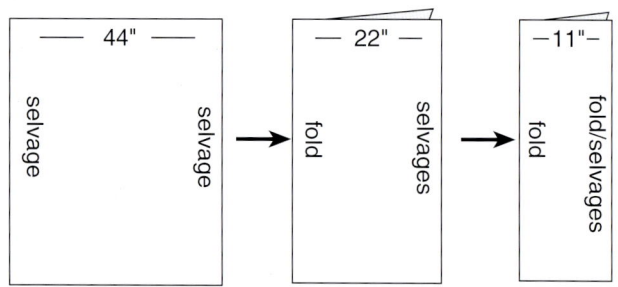

GENERAL SUPPLIES:
- Rotary cutter and mat
- Assorted sizes of rotary cutting rulers, including a large square (NOTE: *The bigger the better. I use square rulers in these sizes: 9 1/2", 12 1/2", 15" and 16 1/2". If the blocks you are framing are 8" or smaller, the 12 1/2" ruler is probably large enough, especially if you are doing a Single Twist or a Double Twist.*)
- Iron and ironing board
- Blocks to be framed (any size, square or rectangular)
- Template Plastic, graph paper, sandpaper and glue stick (for Method 3 only)

FABRIC:
Strip Sizes

To cut strips, fold the fabric in half, selvage to selvage. Then fold it in half again. You will be cutting through four layers of fabric. Cut the strips across the grain, from selvage to selvage.

How many strips should you cut to begin this project? This will be determined by variables such as the method you are using, the size of your blocks and whether you're framing them with a Single, Double or Triple Twist. The beauty of working with scrap quilts is that you'll never run out of fabric! Try my plan for "ready strips" outlined in the Cutting Tip (on page 9).

As a guideline for framing four 6" blocks with a

Color

This is a personal decision. Sometimes you may wish to begin with the blocks and select colors which will enhance and complement fabrics used in the blocks. Other times you may decide to ignore the colors in the blocks altogether and choose fabrics according to what makes you happy. I've worked successfully both ways.

The Ohio Star blocks in "Saturday Night Live" (page 21) are an example of choosing fabric the second way. I didn't like the fabrics in the blocks, except maybe the muslin backgrounds! So the fabric selections for the framing strips were based totally on colors I liked. "Saturday Night Live" is a Triple Twist. Rounds 1 and 3 were stitched using 3 1/2" strips. Round 2 was completed with narrower 2 1/2" strips because the fabric is the lightest and brightest.

When cutting strips to begin the project, be sure to select a variety. Pull lots of different fabrics together and just stack them up. Study the pile, looking for different print scales. Be sure to include some fabrics with multiple colors and some tone-on-tone prints. Look for fabrics that have similar value, but aren't so much alike you can't tell them apart. It doesn't make sense to use 80 different fabrics if it looks like you only used eight!

I consider color a friend, so I've never been particularly afraid of it. My attitude is simple. If I like certain colors together, then they must go together. This security comes from remembering that when making a quilt I am only trying to please myself. Color becomes challenging when you try to create something you think others will like. This task is self-defeating because we can never get inside someone else's head !

Trust your instincts. Learn to cut fabric without worrying about wasting it. I cut lots of strips I may not use for this particular project. My thought? Not to worry! There will be another quilt, and another and another. What doesn't work for this project may be perfect for the next one.

Much of using color successfully is learning to relax and loosen up. Many quilters worry too much. Life is too short to spend time fretting over whether this is the right shade of green or if you'd rather have blue. My advice? Cut the fabric! Remember, there's always more at the quilt shop if you should somehow manage to use up everything you now own.

BLOCK PREPARATION:

Make sure the blocks to be framed are pressed, loose threads are clipped and outer edges are evened up if necessary. Taking a few minutes to do these things before framing them will make better results. Don't worry about making the blocks "perfect." After all, imperfect blocks are one reason for using this framing technique. Neat and tidy counts for a lot, but perfection is for the Deity!

Cutting Tip: *Ready Strips*

Being an obsessive organizer, I am constantly cutting strips and storing them in boxes. I have separate boxes for various strips in widths from 1 1/2" to 3 1/2". That means when beginning a Twist 'n Turn project, I can start with strips already cut.

When I began working on "Starring the Best Friends" (page 10), a box of pastel 3 1/2" strips was ready to work with. No new strips were cut to Twist 'n Turn the blocks for that quilt.

For me, "time" is a four-letter word. Take the opportunity to cut fabric strips when a fabric is on the mat for another project. Store the strips by size and color and they're ready to Twist 'n Turn when you are!

Are you ever too tired to be creative or just not in the mood to sew, yet you want to play with fabric? Why not use those times to cut strips?

Cutting strips is also an excellent way to use up fabrics I call "wonder fabrics"—you wonder why you ever bought them! For projects like this, they can be ideal.

Triangles trimmed from framing strips in "Starring the Best Friends" became Single Twist framing pieces in **"Rosebud Twist."** Sharyn used the Triangle method described in Chapter 3.

A friendship exchange posed the challenge of unifying the 8" blocks in **"Starring the Best Friends"**. Sharyn sewed narrow strips of solid-color fabric to the blocks and then framed them with a Single Twist. She used the rectangle method described in Chapter 2. Never one to waste fabric, she used the triangles trimmed from the framing strips in "Rosebud Twist" (above). The blocks were set together with sashing to add interest and size.

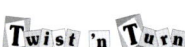

The Gallery

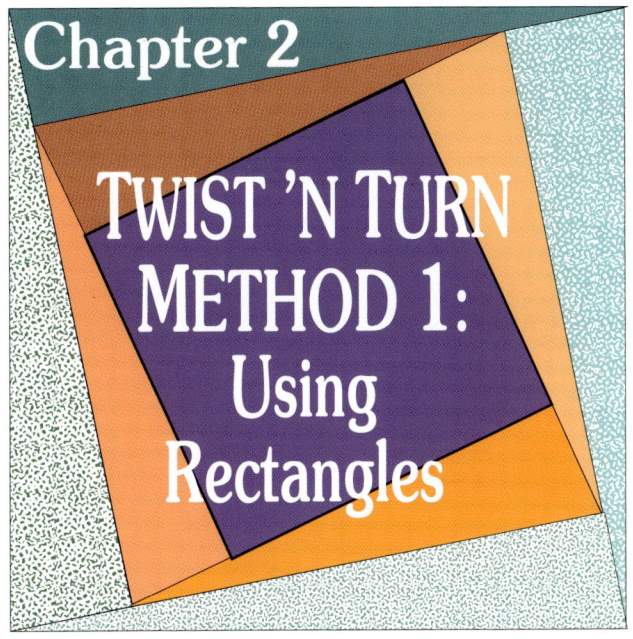

Chapter 2
TWIST 'N TURN METHOD 1: Using Rectangles

In this method, you'll frame blocks using long fabric strips just as they are cut, selvage to selvage. There's no need to measure the blocks or the strips before framing. Not only is using rectangles the easiest of the three Twist 'n Turn methods, it is also the most forgiving of differences in block sizes. When blocks are supposed to be the same size but actually vary, you can make them finish to the same size without hassle, math or worry. Try it and see for yourself!

SEWING A SINGLE TWIST (ROUND 1):

Have your framing strips ready to sew. It's best to keep all the framing strips for a round the same width, either 2 1/2" or 3 1/2".

- Unfold one strip and remove the selvages.
- Place the strip on the block, right sides together, so that the corner of the block lines up with the end of the strip.
- Begin sewing at this corner and sew about half way down the block. This first seam will always be a partial seam (denoted in diagrams by P.S.). Although the first strip is long, leave the excess for now.
- Open the strip and finger press the seam allowance toward the strip.

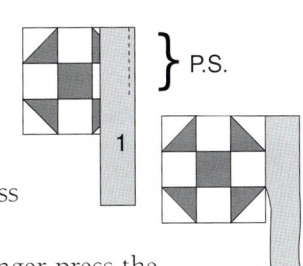

- Unfold the second strip and remove the selvage.
- Place the strip on the block and the first strip, right sides together.
- Sew, starting from the edge of the first framing strip and ending at the corner of the block.
- Trim the second strip even with the edge of the block. Open and finger press.

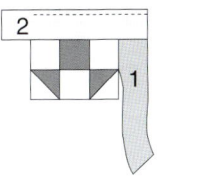 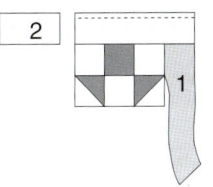 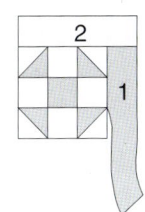

- Repeat with the third and fourth strips, as shown. Be sure to move the first strip out of the way when trimming the fourth one.

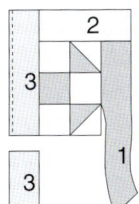 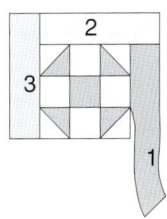 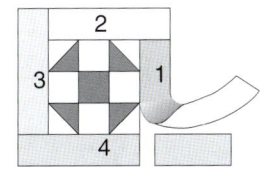

- Place the first strip on the block, right sides together. Complete the seam, stitching to the edge of the fourth strip. Trim the strip even with the edge of the fourth strip. Open and press the block.

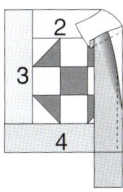 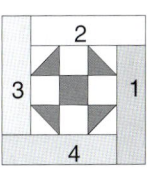

- Now you'll twist the center block and square the framed block using a square ruler. Position the ruler on the framed block at an angle and with the corners intersecting the seamlines, as shown. Trim around the ruler, making a framed block that looks like the one in the diagram. This block twists to the left. For blocks that twist to the right, see "Controlling the Twist" (on page 15).

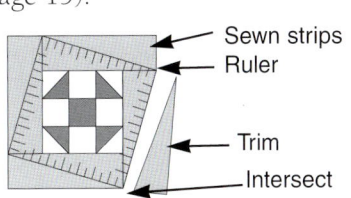
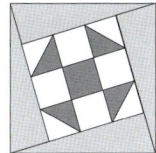

TWIST 'N TURN METHOD 1: Using Rectangles   11

Recycling Tip: No Waste, No Way! *While the triangles you trimmed are not big enough to frame another block the same size, they can be used to frame smaller blocks. So don't throw them away! Place them in a box marked "Twist 'n Turn Triangles." You never know when you might need them!*

I stitched the 8" blocks in "Starring the Best Friends" (page 10) using Method 1. Then I used the triangles to frame the 6" blocks in "Rosebud Twist" (page 10, using Method 2. A perfect solution!

SEWING A DOUBLE OR TRIPLE TWIST (ROUNDS 2 AND 3):

• Sewing one round of strips to the four sides of the block created a Single Twist. To sew a Double Twist, sew a second round of strips to the sides of the block in the same manner as the first, starting in the same corner. Trim the block, using a square ruler as before.

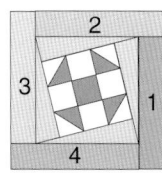 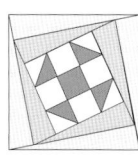

• To sew a Triple Twist, sew a third round of strips to the block, starting in the same corner. Trim the block as before.

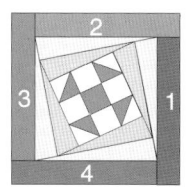 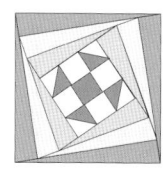

SUMMARY OF PROS AND CONS FOR METHOD 1:

Pros:
- It's easy
- It's forgiving of varying block sizes
- There's no math involved

Cons:
- It has the most fabric waste of the three methods.
- Bias ends up on the outside edge of the block. (NOTE: *As long as you press the block well before squaring it, the danger of the bias stretching is minimized because you won't be handling it much. Keep in mind the edges do not have a 45° angle and are not true bias. One plus of having bias in this position is that there is less fraying of the block's outer edges.*)

Controlling the Twist in Method 1

If you sewed strips to the original block as described in the directions, the block will twist to the left after trimming, as shown. If you want it to twist to the right, place the first framing strip in the opposite corner and sew the partial seam, as shown. Then add strips in a clockwise direction.

You may wish to alternate the twist in an orderly fashion—left, right, left, right. Perhaps you would prefer to sew blocks that twist in the same direction (see "Old Shoes" on page 29.) Or you could whimsically twist the blocks without worrying about controlling the direction, as in "Celebration" (page 17).

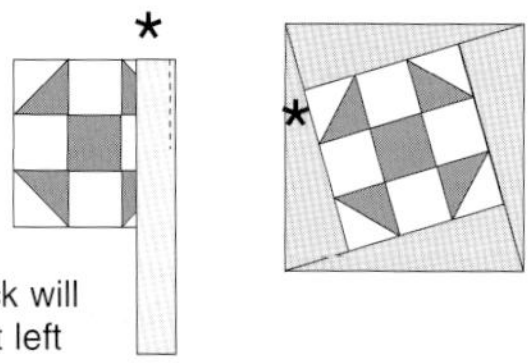

LEFT CORNER — Block will twist left

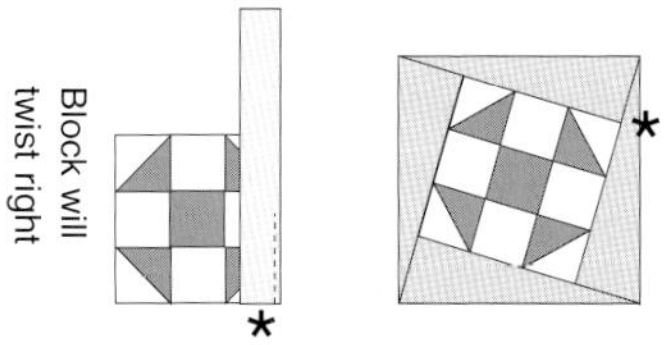

Block will twist right — RIGHT CORNER

Sharyn created color-full zig-zags by carefully placing colors in the framing triangles of **"Pinwheel Twist."** Notice the borders. They're made by framing the entire quilt top in a Single Twist. Anything is possible with Twist 'n Turn!

Sharyn controlled the twist through color and setting in **"Asilomar Sampler."** The blocks, presented to Sharyn by friends, were perfect for the Twist 'n Turn. Sharyn says, "Suddenly it didn't matter that the blocks were not all the same size, color or fabric."

Twist 'n Turn

The Gallery 13

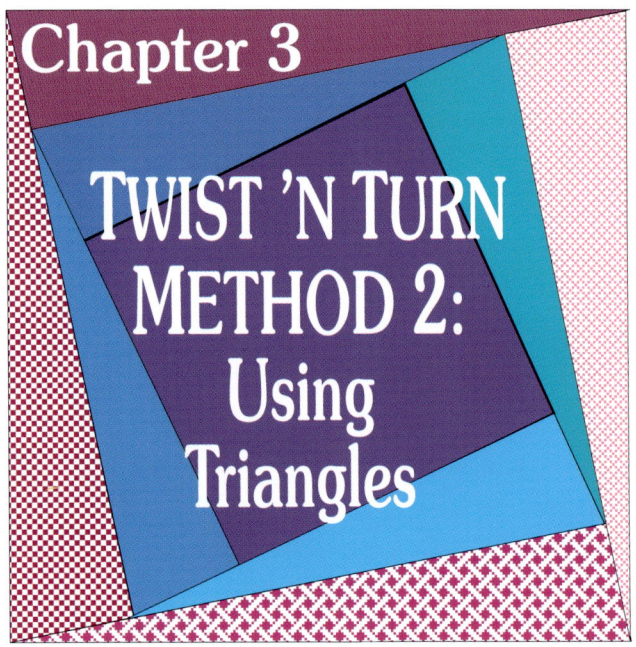

Chapter 3

TWIST 'N TURN METHOD 2: Using Triangles

In this method you'll use the tiniest bit of math. Don't let that put you off—I promise it's not difficult. Simple addition is all there is to it!

If you are framing blocks of different sizes, start with one of the largest ones. If the variation in block sizes is less than 1", then the same calculation you use for the largest block will work for the smaller ones. If block sizes vary more than 1", you'll need to do the math for smaller sizes as well. Again, remember to use the same width strips in a round. Either 2 1/2" or 3 1/2" strips work well for this method.

DETERMINING STRIP SIZES FOR A SINGLE TWIST:
- Measure the block, raw edge to raw edge.
- Add 5 1/2" to the block measurement. (That's all the math involved. Not bad, wouldn't you say?) We'll call this sum "X."

Example: BLOCK SIZE + ADD-ON = SUM
           6 1/2"   + 5 1/2" = 12"

Therefore, "X" = 12"

- Take four framing strips and unfold each one once. Stack them one on top of another, open edges together. There will be 8 layers of fabric. Remove the selvages.

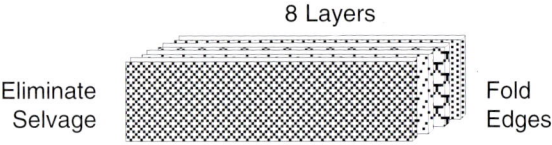

- Measure "X" on the strip from the open ends and cut through all layers, as shown.

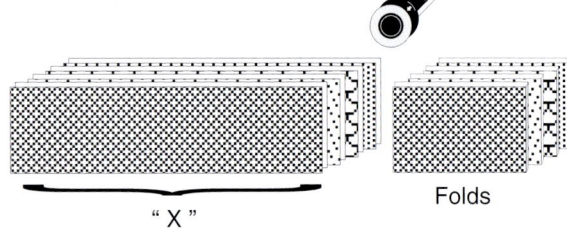

- Slice the layers corner to corner once, as shown.

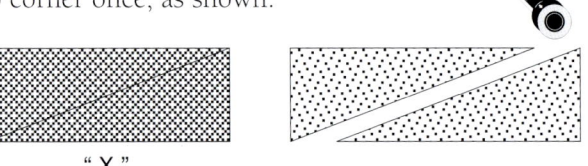

- Separate the resulting triangles into two piles with right sides up and square corners. There will be 8 Left Corner triangles and 8 Right Corner triangles. Now make two piles, each containing four Left Corner Triangles, and two containing four Right Corner triangles, as shown.

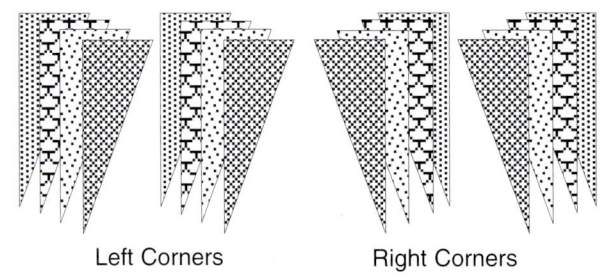

SEWING A SINGLE TWIST (ROUND 1):
- Begin with one pile of four Left Corner triangles.

Reminder: *Be sure to always sew the first triangle with a partial seam starting from the square corner.*

Set aside the other three piles for now. You will use them to frame three more blocks. Place the first triangle on the block, right sides together. Sew a partial seam (P.S.) from the corner.

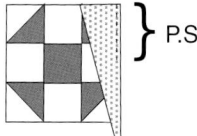 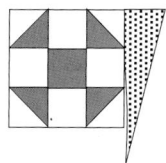

- Open and finger press the seam allowance toward the triangle.
- Place the second triangle on the block, right sides together, and stitch, as shown. Open and finger press the seam allowance. Don't be alarmed by the long, skinny point of the triangle at the end of each seam. You'll trim them when you square the block. That's why the extra inches are added in the calculations.

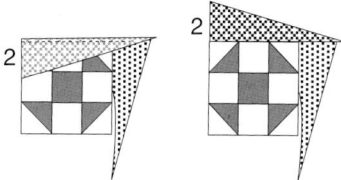

- Sew the remaining two triangles to the block, one at a time, to complete the first round, as shown.

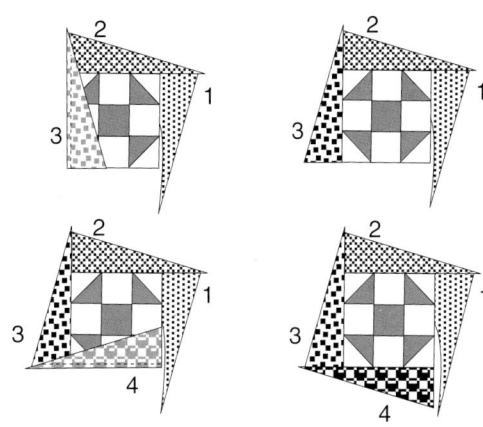

Controlling the Twist in Method 2

Left Corner triangles will twist the blocks to the left. Right Corner triangles will twist them to the right.

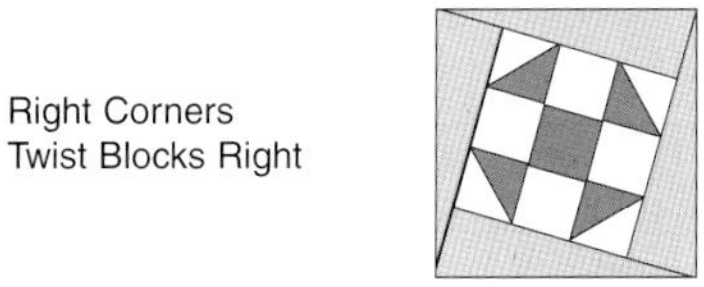

Right Corners Twist Blocks Right

Cutting folded strips will automatically produce triangles for both left and right twists. If you want all the blocks to twist in the same direction, simply unfold all of the strips to a single layer. Then stack them right sides up, measure "X" and cut. Be sure that the corner-to-corner slice is always made in the same direction.

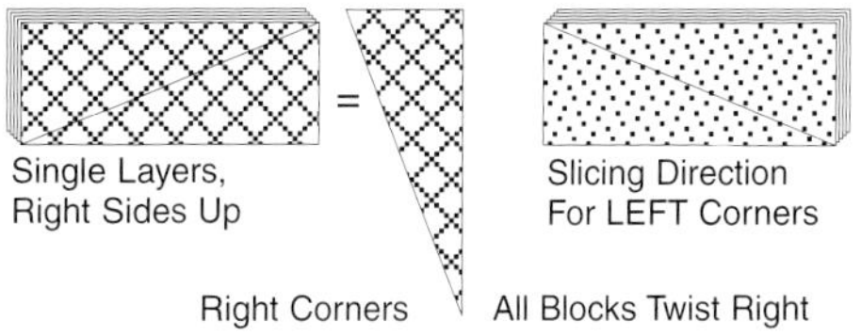

Single Layers, Right Sides Up

Slicing Direction For LEFT Corners

Right Corners   All Blocks Twist Right

Using the instructions provided will provide triangles to frame four blocks—two that twist left and two that twist right. If you want a scrappier look achieved by using different fabric triangles for each block, cut additional rectangles from other fabrics using the "X" measurement. Slice the rectangles, separate and stack them in Left Corner and Right Corner piles as before.

TWIST 'n TURN METHOD 2: *Using Triangles*   15

- Complete the seam on the first triangle. Open and press as before.

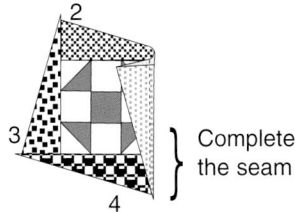

- Use a large square ruler to square the block, even the edges and trim the excess fabric.

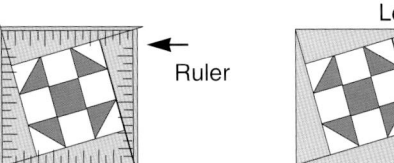

SEWING A DOUBLE OR TRIPLE TWIST (ROUNDS 2 AND 3):

For a Double Twist:

- Measure the framed block from raw edge to raw edge. Add 5 1/2" to arrive at a new "X" number.
- Cut rectangles this size and slice them, stacking the triangles as before.
- Sew left triangles to the sides of the block, joining the first one with a partial seam.
- Complete the seam, press and square the block.

For a Triple Twist:

- Measure the Double Twist block and add 5 1/2" to arrive at a new "X" number.
- Cut rectangles this size. Slice, stack and sew left triangles to the Double Twist block. Press and square the block.

SUMMARY OF PROS AND CONS FOR METHOD 2:

Pros:
- Blocks are easier to square up.
- There's less fabric waste.

Cons:
- It requires some math.
- Bias ends up on the outside of the block. (NOTE: *As described in Method 1, this is not a big problem, especially if the block is pressed well before squaring it.*)

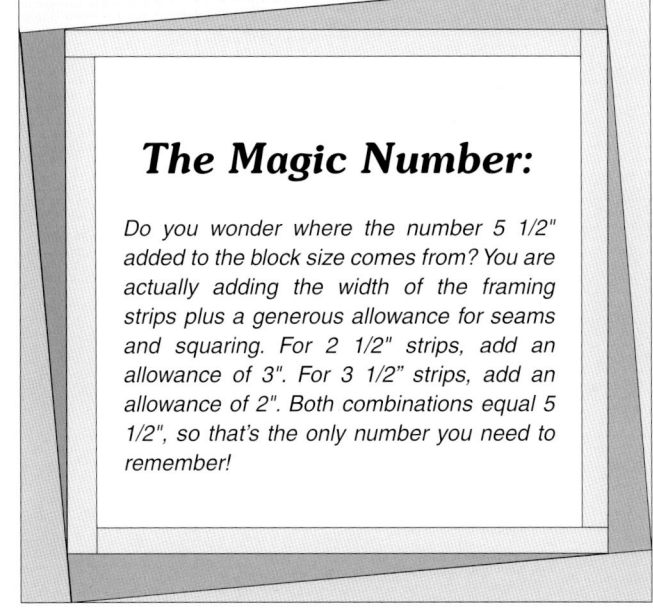

The Magic Number:

Do you wonder where the number 5 1/2" added to the block size comes from? You are actually adding the width of the framing strips plus a generous allowance for seams and squaring. For 2 1/2" strips, add an allowance of 3". For 3 1/2" strips, add an allowance of 2". Both combinations equal 5 1/2", so that's the only number you need to remember!

Imagine!

- What if you combined Single, Double and Triple Twist blocks in the same quilt? This could be an especially interesting choice if the blocks to be framed are a wide range of sizes.
- Normally all the square corners should be at the same position (left or right) on any one block when making Double Twist or Triple Twist blocks. If you twist a block left in the first round and right in the second, it will bring the center block back straight. But what if that's what you want to do? (See blocks in Linda Hamby's "Halloween Sampler" on page 21).

Twelve quilting buddies personalized the doll blocks (a *Quiltmaker* design) in **"My Quilting Friends."** Sharyn found that rectangular blocks are a bit trickier to frame, but definitely worth the effort. She framed the blocks with three rounds of straight strips before twisting them.

Randomly twisted 12" Star blocks seem to dance across the surface of **"Celebration."** Sashing provides a resting place between the vibrant blocks. At first Sharyn thought the blocks were too strong to use together, but Twist 'n Turn unified them.

The Gallery 17

Chapter 4
TWIST 'N TURN METHOD 3: Using Templates

You'll need some knowledge of drafting and template making for this method. It's a good choice when all the blocks are the same or nearly the same size. If the blocks vary widely, you'll need to make several templates for the different sizes. If this is the case, you might prefer Method 1 or 2, the no-template methods. Using a template lets you cut the framing triangles so the straight grain will end up on the outer edge of the block. Also, you won't need to square the block with a ruler because you'll cut right-size framing triangles for each round.

SUPPLIES:
- Graph paper
- Ruler
- Pencil
- Heavyweight translucent plastic template material
- Glue stick
- Fine sandpaper
- Craft scissors for cutting paper and plastic

MAKING TEMPLATES:
First you need to decide how much you wish to add to the original block size. Study the drawing for the framed block. Each framing triangle has three sides, labeled A, B and C. Notice that:
- The shortest side of the triangle is A. It represents the approximate size increase. As a guideline, try a 2" increase for a 6" block.
- B is the sum of the finished original block size plus A. For example, using the guideline for a 6" block, B = 6" + 2" or 8".

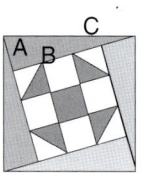

To draft a pattern piece:
- Draw a line on graph paper equal in length to B.
- At one end, draw a line equal in length to A and perpendicular to B.
- Now draw C, a line connecting the ends of A and B.
- Add a 1/4" seam allowance around the triangle to complete the pattern piece. Blunt the pattern piece 1/4" from the point if you wish. Mark the grainline parallel to C.

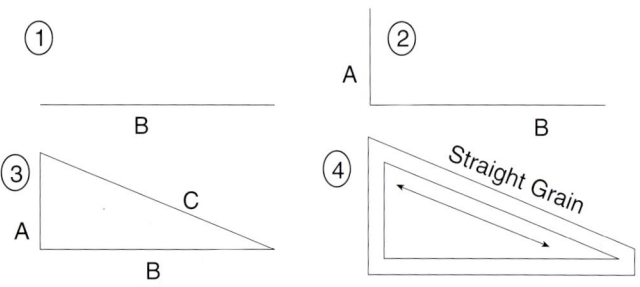

To make a template "sandwich":
- Glue heavy, translucent template plastic to the right side of the pattern piece.
- Turn the pattern piece over and dab more glue around the edges of the triangle.
- Place a piece of heavyweight sandpaper on the glue, rough side out.
- Let the three layers dry for about 10 minutes

Hint: Another of my favorite template methods is John Flynn's Cut Your Own Template Kit®. Cut the paper pattern piece out and glue it to the colored side of the template material. Then use the special cutter which comes in the kit to cut the template easily. It is impossible to cut the template with a rotary cutter, which makes it ideal for cutting Twist 'n Turn triangles from fabric strips. Check your local quilt shop or order from Chitra Publications by calling (800)-628-8244.

before cutting out the template through all three layers. If the glue isn't dry before cutting, the layers may shift. Templates made this way are durable enough to use with the rotary cutter.

CUTTING FABRIC STRIPS AND TRIANGLES:
- To determine the width of strips to cut, position the template on a rotary cutting ruler, placing C along the outside edge of the ruler.

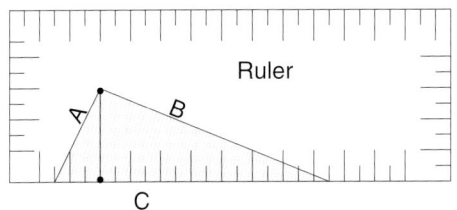

- Measure as shown and add a small "safety margin" to that number. Then cut selvage-to-selvage strips as wide as this measurement.
- Place the template on the strips and cut around them using your rotary cutter and ruler.
- Remember this is a directional template. If you are cutting through two layers of fabric at one time, place them wrong sides together to yield both Right Corner triangles and Left Corner triangles. For the block to twist left, sew four Left Corner triangles to it. Sew Right Corner triangles for the block to twist right.

SEWING A SINGLE TWIST (ROUND 1):
- Place the first triangle on the block, right sides together. Sew a partial seam from the corner.
- Open and finger press the seam allowance toward the triangle.
- Place the second triangle on the block, right sides together and stitch. Open and finger press the seam allowance.
- Sew the remaining two triangles one at a time to complete the first round.
- Complete the seam on the first triangle and press the block. There is no need to square it because you cut accurate pieces with templates.

SEWING A DOUBLE OR TRIPLE TWIST (ROUNDS 2 AND 3):
For a Double Twist:
- Decide on the amount of increase you want to add in the second round (A). Measure the framed Single Twist block (B).
- Make a new template using these numbers. Measure the template as before to determine the strip width.
- Cut triangles and sew them to the sides of the block, beginning with a partial seam for the first triangle.
- Complete the partial seam and press the block.

For a Triple Twist:
- Decide on the amount of increase you want in the third round (A). Measure the framed Double Twist block (B).
- Make a new template using these numbers and use it to determine the strip width.
- Cut triangles and sew them to the sides of the block as before to complete the Triple Twist.
- Complete the partial seam and press the block.

SUMMARY OF PROS AND CONS FOR METHOD 3:
Pros:
- There's the least fabric waste of the three methods.
- Straight grain ends up on the outside edge of the block.

Cons:
- Starting blocks need to be the same or nearly the same size.
- It's not as forgiving of size differences as the other two no-template methods.
- It requires the additional step of making templates.

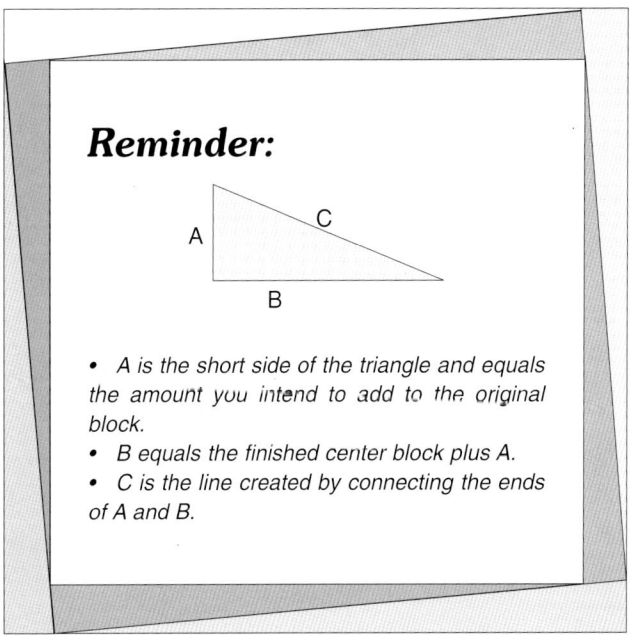

Reminder:
- A is the short side of the triangle and equals the amount you intend to add to the original block.
- B equals the finished center block plus A.
- C is the line created by connecting the ends of A and B.

Sharyn learned a value lesson when framing **Fan blocks**. Because the block is dark on two sides and light on the other two, the dark side got "lost" when she used dark framing pieces. She solved the problem by sewing light strips to the dark sides before twisting the block.

Arlene Stamper of San Diego, California, set friendship blocks with a Single Twist in **"Ode to Shirley Valentine."**

20   *The Gallery*

Linda Hamby of Encinitas, California, took part in a Halloween friendship swap that required blocks in any size as long as it was a multiple of 3". That provided the extra challenge of combining square and rectangular blocks in a quilt. Twist 'n Turn to the rescue! Linda's **Halloween Sampler** illustrates how blocks in a Triple Twist can remain upright by twisting left and right in the same block.

Leftover Ohio Star blocks found a home in **"Saturday Night Live,"** the first Triple Twist Sharyn made. She waited 10 years before attempting to use the blocks in a quilt and says, "I couldn't be happier with the results!"

Chapter 5

A Triple Twist Exercise

This Triple Twist Exercise is an excellent choice for your first Twist 'n Turn project. Because it combines both Method 1 and Method 2, using both rectangles and triangles, after twisting as few as four blocks you'll have a feel for which method you prefer.

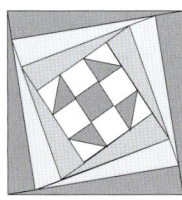

The directions that follow provide an efficient use of fabric. The usual waste triangles trimmed from the blocks in Method 1, which is the technique we will be using on the third round, become the first round triangles on the next block!

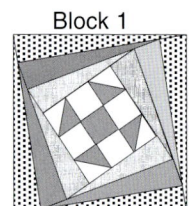
Block 1

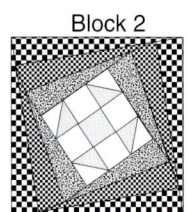
Block 2

I use Method 1 for the third round because it is the most forgiving of the three methods. This means greater ease in getting all blocks to end up the same size. And that makes them much easier to set together in a quilt!

GETTING STARTED:

For the Triple Twist Exercise I recommend framing blocks that are smaller than 8". Because they will roughly double in size by the time you add three rounds of framing pieces, using larger blocks could mean "outgrowing" any square ruler currently available. Then squaring the blocks would be difficult.

Use four blocks so you can twist two to the left and two to the right. Four blocks will make a small wall quilt or even a small crib or lap quilt.

You will want assorted strips in both 3 1/2" and 2 1/2" widths. The 3 1/2" strips will be used in the first and third rounds. I recommend that they be similar in value and color, value being the most important. The 2 1/2" strips are used in the second round. Think of this round as the accent round. Choose a light value or bright fabric for these strips. Usually you'll need less of an accent fabric so that's why I suggest using 2 1/2" strips here.

SEWING ROUND 1:

• Select four different 3 1/2" strips and unfold each one once. Stack them one on top of another, open edges together. There will be 8 layers of fabric. Remove the selvages.

• Determine the "X" number for your blocks as described in Method 2. (Remember "X" = the unfinished block size + 5 1/2".)

• Measure "X" on the strip from the open ends and cut through all layers, as shown. Set the remaining strips (with the folded edges) aside to use later in Round 3.

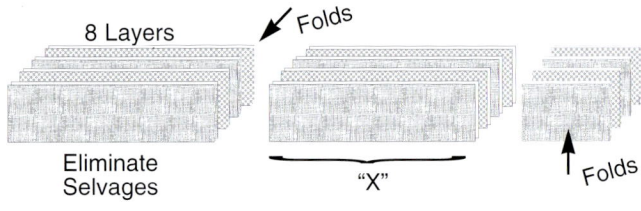

• Slice the layers corner to corner once, as shown. Set half of the triangles aside for another project.

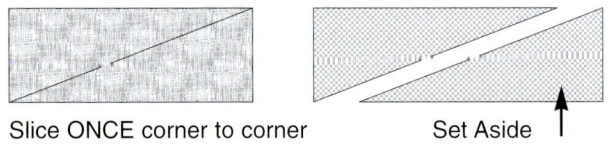

• Separate the triangles into two piles, matching the square corners. There will be 4 Left Corner triangles and 4 Right Corner triangles. Set the Right Corner triangles aside for now.

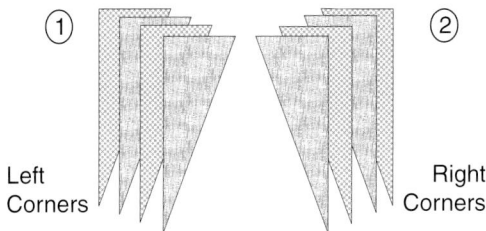

- Begin with the pile of Left Corner triangles. Place the first triangle on the block, right sides together. Sew a partial seam from the corner.

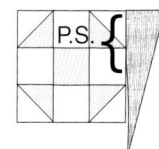

- Open and finger press the seam allowance toward the triangle.
- Place the second triangle on the block, right sides together, and stitch. Open and finger press the seam allowance. Remember, you'll trim the excess when you square the block.

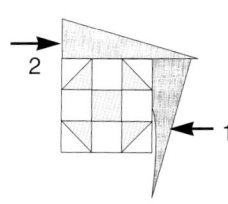

- Sew the remaining two triangles to the remaining sides of the block one at a time to complete the first round.

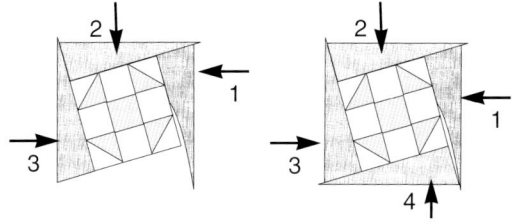

- Complete the seam on the first triangle. Finger press open as before.
- Press the block. 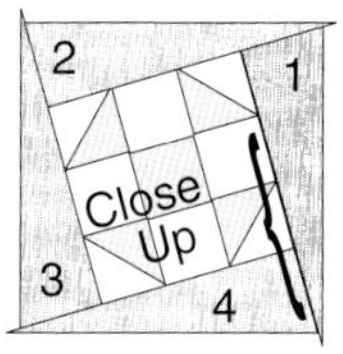
- Use one of the large square rulers to square the block. At this point you have an option. You can cut the four blocks the same size or vary them. It isn't until Round 3 that you will need to make sure the blocks are equal in size. As a general guide, I anticipate that the block I square up now will be roughly 2" larger than the one I began with. This means that my 6" block may now be 8" or 8 1/2". I can cut it either size.

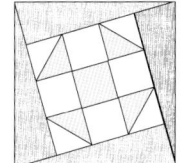

- Notice that the center block is now twisted to the left.

SEWING ROUND 2:

- Select four different 2 1/2" framing strips and unfold each one once. Stack them one on top of another, open edges together. There will be 8 layers of fabric. Remove the selvages.
- Determine the "X" number for your blocks as described in Method 2. (This time "X" = the new block size + 5 1/2".)
- Measure "X" on the strip from the open ends and cut through all layers.
- Slice the layers corner to corner once, as shown. 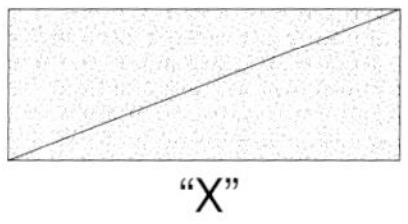
- Separate the triangles into two piles, matching the square corners. There will be 8 Left Corner triangles and 8 Right Corner triangles. Now make two piles containing four Left Corner Triangles each and two piles containing four Right Corner triangles each, as shown. Each pile should have four different fabrics.

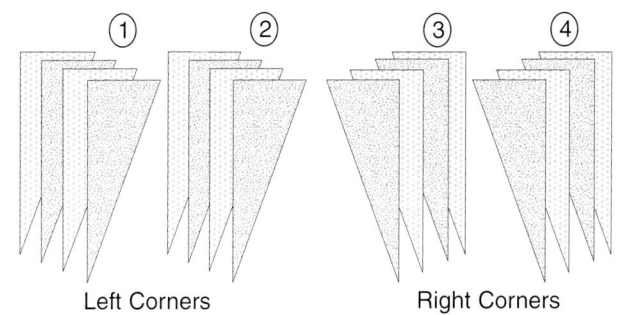

- Begin with one pile of four Left Corner triangles. Set aside the other three piles for now. Place the first triangle on the block, right sides together and corners aligned. The wide end of the triangle for Round 2 should always be sewn to the wide end of of the triangle in Round 1. Stitch a partial seam. Open and finger press the seam allowance.
- Sew the remaining triangles to the remaining sides of the block, one at a time.
- Complete the partial seam and finger press open as before.
- Press the block. Use one of the large square rulers to square the block to the desired size. Again, the block size will increase by roughly 2".

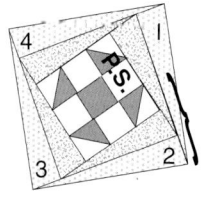

SEWING ROUND 3:

- Take the 3 1/2" strips you set aside in Round 1.

Place one strip on the block, right sides together, so that the corner of the block (the wide end of the triangle from Round 2) lines up with the end of the strip.
• Begin sewing at this corner and sew a partial seam.
• Open the strip and finger press the seam allowance toward the strip.
• Place the second 3 1/2" strip on the block and the first strip, right sides together. Sew, starting from the corner of the first framing strip and ending in the corner of the block.
• Trim the second strip even with the edge of the block. Open and finger press.
• Repeat with the third and fourth 3 1/2" strips, as shown. Be sure to move the first strip out of the way when trimming the fourth one.
• Complete the seam on the first strip. Trim the strip even with the edge of the fourth strip. Press the block.

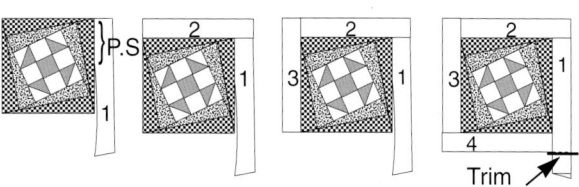

• Square the block to desired size, setting aside the triangles you trim off as excess. This is the finished size for all of the blocks. When in doubt, square the block a bit larger than you think it needs to be. You can always trim it down later, but if this first block is smaller than remaining ones, using it with others in the quilt will be difficult.

Hint: *Unfold and stack leftover pieces from the 2 1/2" strips. You can use them later to cut additional rectangles for other projects or use them if you want to frame more than four blocks. When cutting additional rectangles from these pieces, be sure to position four strips right side up and four more wrong side up to ensure cutting both Left and Right Corners.*

FRAMING THE REMAINING BLOCKS:
• Take the triangles leftover from trimming Round 3 of the first block. Sew them to the second block, using the directions given in Sewing Round 1.
• Cut triangles from 2 1/2" accent strips and sew them to the block for Round 2 as before.
• Use 3 1/2" strips for Round 3 and complete the second block.
• These two blocks twist to the left. If you want all of the blocks to twist left, continue sewing the triangles trimmed from Round 3 strips in Round 1 of the next block. If you want blocks to twist right, take the Right Corner triangles you set aside in Round 1 of the first block. Use them for Round 1 of the third block.
• Add Rounds 2 and 3 to the third block, using triangles cut from 2 1/2" accent strips and 3 1/2" strips as before.
• Trim the third block and use the triangles for Round 1 of the fourth block. Add Rounds 2 and 3 as you did for the third block.
• Set your four Twist 'n Turn blocks in a quilt top. Layer the top with backing and batting. Quilt as desired and bind using your favorite method.

Reminders:
•*Always start sewing from the square corner of the triangle.*
•*Always sew the first triangle with a partial seam.*
•*When switching directions from left twisting block to right, it may feel a bit awkward at first. But you'll soon get the hang of it.*
•*The bright or light accent fabric is always in the Twist 2 position and usually cut from narrower strips.*
•*You can use leftover triangles from Round 3 for Round 1 of the next block, providing you want the next one to twist in the same direction.*
•*Left Corners will twist a block left. Right Corners will twist a block right.*

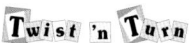

"Wild Crows" is the result of a block-of-the-month drawing won by Brigitte Palmer. Because the blocks were large, she framed them with a Double Twist and used straight strips for sashing.

Linda Packer "saved" these **circa 1950 blocks** with Twist 'n Turn. She bought them at an auction without seeing all of them. They turned out to be distorted and had sat in a drawer for years. Colorful framing pieces make the finished quilt fairly sing with success!

The Gallery

Sharyn's **Halloween quilt** shows how Twist 'n Turn blocks can be used with unframed ones. Try combining the technique with unframed blocks in your design. "You are in control. Use the method wherever it works," reminds Sharyn.

A Single Twist was Sandy Andersen's choice for her **House quilt**. The El Cajon, California, quilter achieved the illusion of rolling hillsides with blue framing pieces on three sides and green on the bottom. The horizontal sashing creates a road complete with a white line and adds to the neighborhood feel of the quilt.

26   The Gallery

Chapter 6
Some Thoughts On Setting

Any straight or diagonal settings you use with regular blocks can be used with Twist 'n Turn framed blocks. Here are a few ideas:
- Tangent Sets: set block-to-block
- Alternating Sets: plain squares or secondary blocks are used between the Twist 'n Turn blocks
- Sashed Set: Twist 'n Turn blocks are separated by fabric strips in either contrasting or muted colors

Setting blocks with the Twist 'n Turn will give you an incredible amount of freedom to be as creative and individualistic as you dare to be! I find myself wanting to set all my blocks this way now. I know that eventually that would become boring, but so far I have made no two quilts alike. Neither have the quiltmakers whose work is featured in this book.

The challenge now is coming up with more ideas using the concept. I might sew straight framing strips to blocks before twisting them, or maybe after! Keep in mind that not all the blocks in your quilt have to be framed with Twist 'n Turn. If you study my Halloween quilt (page 26), you will see that not all of the blocks are twisted. This is an example of uncontrolled "twisting" in which I made no attempt to organize the way the blocks twisted. I first put all of the blocks up on the flannel wall. They ranged in size from 6" square to 9" x 12". I moved them around to "balance" their sizes and colors. There were obvious holes which needed to be filled. A 9" block could easily finish at 12" with Twist 'n Turn. The rectangles took a bit more manipulation, but I knew if the finished block stayed a multiple of 3", then I could fit everything together in the end. Some blocks I cut down from the original size and then framed. Some I cut down and did not frame. The bat which is appliquéd to the upper right corner was originally appliquéd to a 6" x 9" rectangle of black print fabric. When I found I would need to eliminate one block, this solution was so perfect it felt like it was planned that way from the beginning! The blocks were part of a friendship exchange which is always challenging. Giving yourself permission to do whatever is necessary to the blocks to make them work can be quite liberating!

I must always keep trying to make each quilt something unique, if only for my own satisfaction. I have finished more quilts in just a few months while working on this concept than I would have dared hope I could. Quite honestly, many of them might never have been finished any other way. In some cases I felt the blocks were beyond saving. Now I truly believe that Twist 'n Turn framing can save any block.

Some work better than others…

Having said that, let's look at some ways Twist 'n Turn quilts could have been more successful. Using a Triple Twist for the House blocks in my "Northridge" quilt, shown in this chapter, was a bit too much. It didn't start out to be an earthquake quilt, but you can't live in southern California as long as I have without looking at this quilt and immediately thinking of the devastating 1994 event in Northridge. On the other hand, Sandy Andersen's delightful little House Quilt (page 26) framed with a Single Twist is very successful. It helped keep the houses upright! Also, using green framing pieces on the bottom and blue on three sides was ingenious. Instead of feeling like the houses are about to topple over, her quilt creates

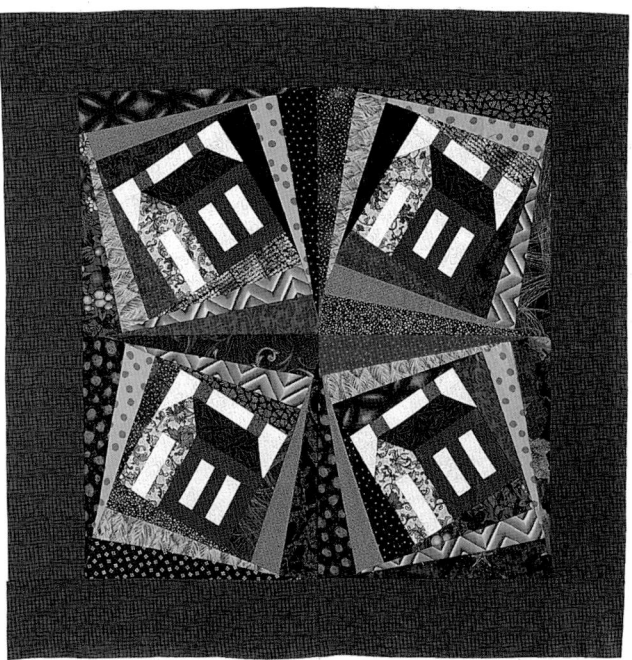

Sharyn says, "A Triple Twist proved to be too much for these House blocks!" As a Californian, the quilt makes her think of the 1994 earthquake, hence the name **"Northridge."** She suggests a better solution would have been framing the blocks with a Single Twist as in the House quilt on page 26.

Barbara Hutchins of Santee, California, made this quilt which illustrates the importance of print scale and value when using the Twist 'n Turn technique. She began framing squares of a novelty print that featured cute dogs and fire hydrants. However, the busy print in the sashing makes it difficult to see the details.

the comfortable illusion of rolling hills.

Barbara Hutchin's little fire hydrant quilt, shown here, is another example of a quilt which doesn't quite hit the mark. Because of the very busy sashing fabric, all of the cute details are overshadowed. When she showed me the quilt her first words were, "You're probably not going to want to use this one." However, I believe, and Barbara agrees, that there are valuable lessons to be learned from such "mistakes."

How many blocks?

You can frame any number of blocks. If you want to keep a balance of blocks that twist left and right, you'll need to frame an even number of blocks. For example, you could set 16 blocks in four rows of four blocks.

You can use odd numbers, but they will not "finish the twist" in a balanced way. In a nine-block quilt with blocks that twist both left and right, you'll have five of one and four of the other. "Saturday Night Live" (page 21) is an example of this. There are 15 blocks set in three rows of five. I was more concerned with the intensity of the yellow around the blocks being balanced than I was with balancing the twist.

Ready, set... twist!

I want you to be successful and I want you to have fun, so I encourage you to "practice" the technique on blocks you aren't emotionally invested in first. Then work with those very special blocks you've been saving for just the right quilt. Who knows, even the practice blocks could end up as a spectacular quilt! Twist 'n Turn framing works on other things besides pieced and appliquéd blocks. For example, why not frame some cross stitch or stencilled blocks? Or, how about those old lace doilies you've been collecting? Novelty print squares work well, too. By now, I trust your creative juices are in full swing and your fingers are itching to cut fabric. So let's start twistin'!

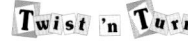

Tiny 3" Shoofly blocks found new life with Twist 'n Turn. All 16 blocks in **"Old Shoes"** (right) twist left. Sharyn chose dark values and low intensity fabrics for the framing strips. A single fabric frames each block. Compare the feel of this quilt with **"New Shoes"** (below). It's the same block but they Twist 'n Turn left and right. There's more variety in fabrics used for framing, too.

Chapter 7

TWIST 'N TURN BLOCK LIBRARY

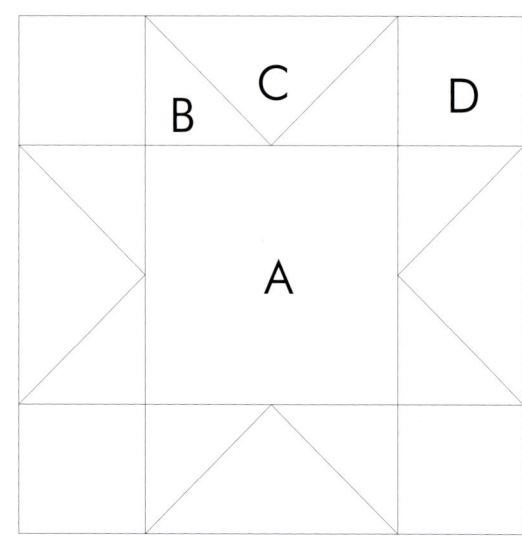

6" Sawtooth Star Templates

If you don't already have a closet, drawer or box full of blocks which have never been set into a finished quilt, these 6" blocks may help you get started. The pattern pieces are for 6" finished sizes because each round of framing pieces you add increases the size of your finished block. Unless your goal is a very large finished quilt, I recommend using blocks less than 10".

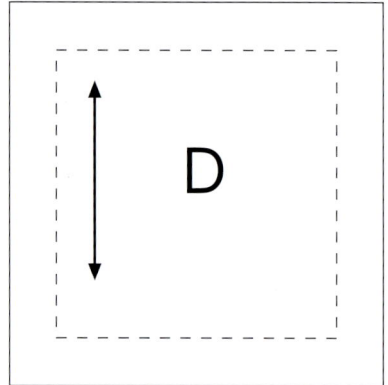

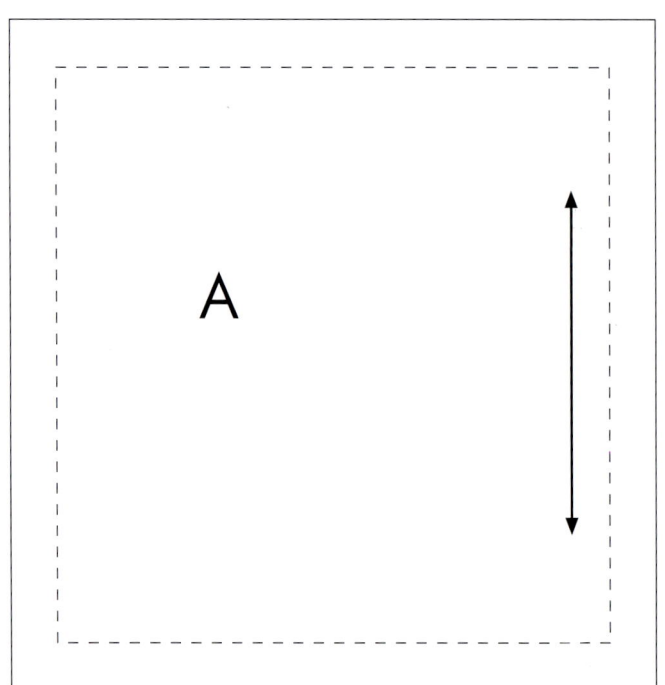

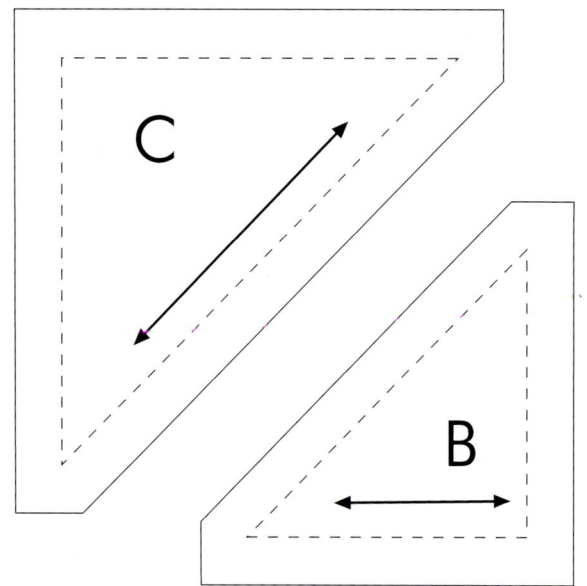

30 TWIST 'n TURN Block Pattern Library

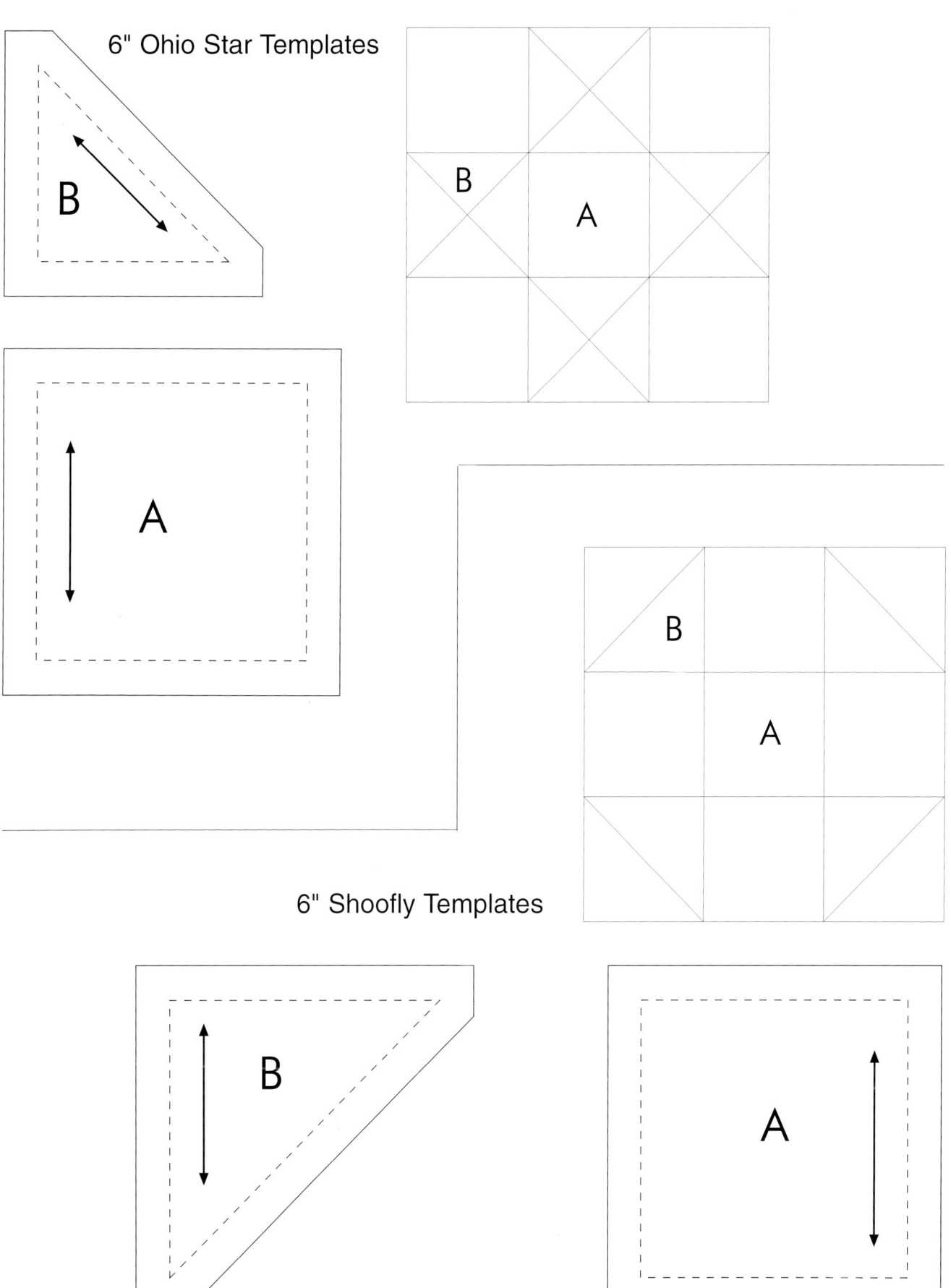

TWIST 'n TURN Block Pattern Library

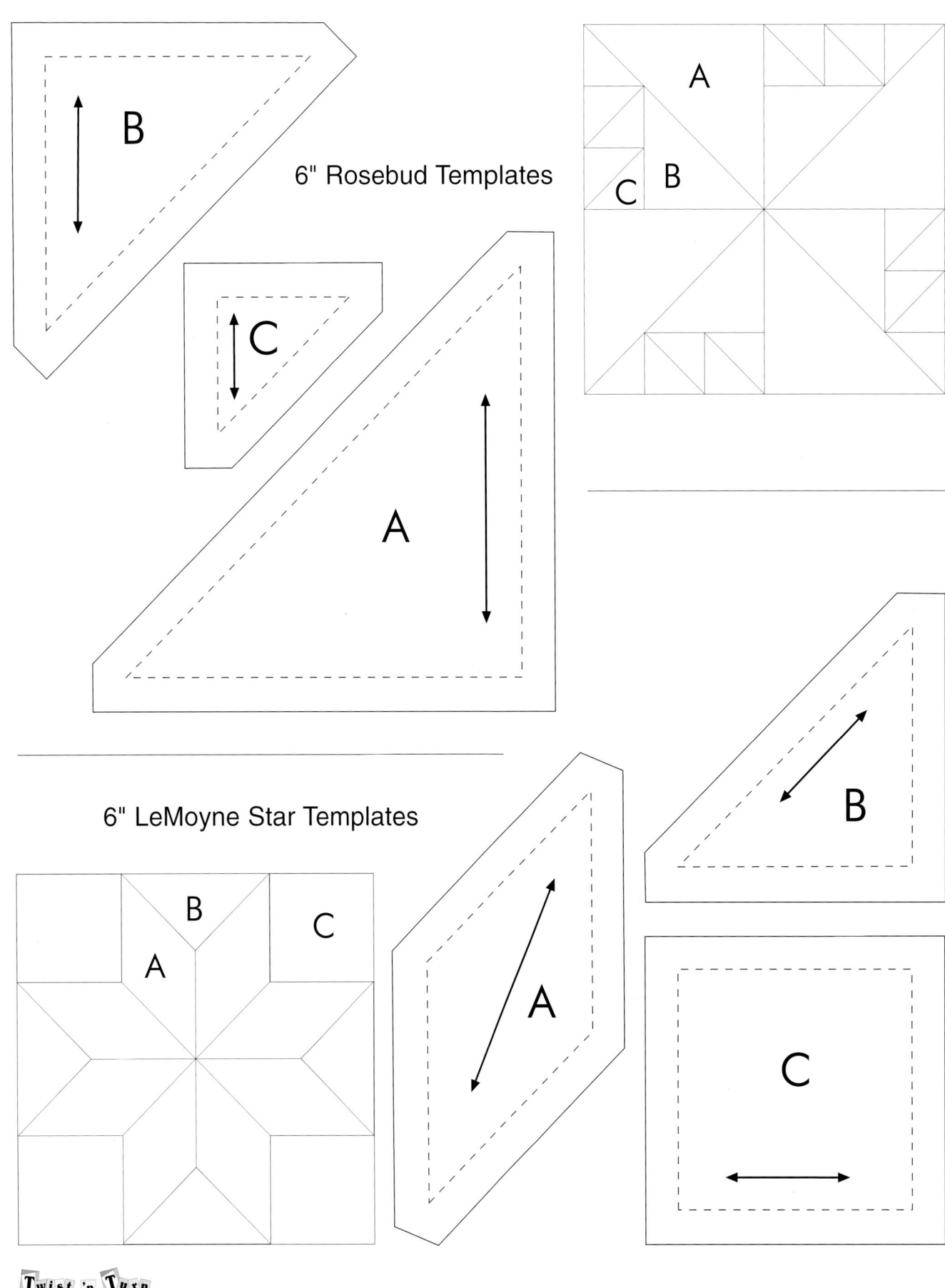